~A BINGO BOOK~

Elements
(and Types)
of Poetry
Bingo Book

COMPLETE BINGO GAME IN A BOOK

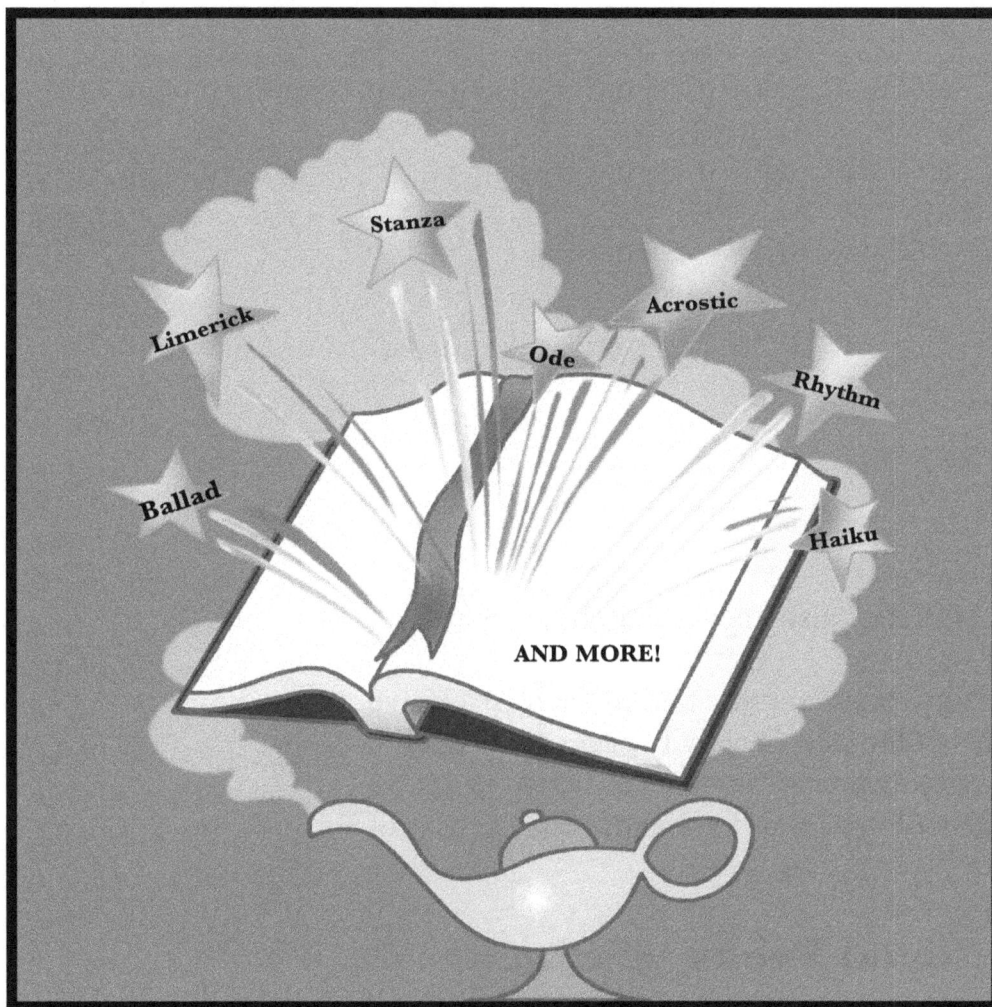

Stanza

Acrostic

Limerick

Ode

Rhythm

Ballad

Haiku

AND MORE!

Written By Rebecca Stark
Educational Books 'n' Bingo

TITLE: Elements (and forms) of Poetry Bingo
AUTHOR: Rebecca Stark

Educational Books 'n' Bingo

ISBN 978-0-87386-486-2

Printed in the U.S.A.

ELEMENTS OF POETRY BINGO DIRECTIONS

INCLUDED:

List of Terms

Templates for Additional Terms and Clues

2 Clues per Term

30 Unique Bingo Cards

Markers

1. **Either cut apart the book or make copies of ALL the sheets. You might want to make an extra copy of the clue sheets to use for introduction and review. Keep the sheets in an envelope for easy reuse.**

2. Cut apart the call cards with terms and clues.

3. Pass out one bingo card per student. There are enough for a class of 30.

4. Pass out markers. You may cut apart the markers included in this book or use any other small items of your choice.

5. Decide whether or not you will require the entire card to be filled. Requiring the entire card to be filled provides a better review. However, if you have a short time to fill, you may prefer to have them do the just the border or some other format. Tell the class before you begin what is required.

6. There are 50 terms. Read the list before you begin. If there are any terms that have not been covered in class, you may want to read to the students the term and clues before you begin.

7. There is a blank space in the middle of each card. You can instruct the students to use it as a free space or you can write in answers to cover terms not included. Of course, in this case you would create your own clues. (Templates provided.)

8. Shuffle the cards and place them in a pile. Two or three clues are provided for each term. If you plan to play the game with the same group more than once, you might want to choose a different clue for each game. If not, you may choose to use more than one clue.

9. Be sure to keep the cards you have used for the present game in a separate pile. When a student calls, "Bingo," he or she will have to verify that the correct answers are on his or her card AND that the markers were placed in response to the proper questions. Pull out the cards that are on the student's card keeping them in the order they were used in the game. Read each clue as it was given and ask the student to identify the correct answer from his or her card.

10. If the student has the correct answers on the card AND has shown that they were marked in response to the *correct questions,* then that student is the winner and the game is over. If the student does not have the correct answers on the card OR he or she marked the answers in response to *the wrong questions*, then the game continues until there is a proper winner.

11. If you want to play again, reshuffle the cards and begin again.

Have fun!

TOPICS INCLUDED

ACROSTIC	METER
ALLEGORY	METONYMY
ALLITERATION	ODE
ALLUSION	ONOMATOPOEIA
ASSONANCE	PARODY
BALLAD	PERSONIFICATION
CAESURA	POET
CINQUAIN	POETRY
CLERIHEW	QUATRAIN
CONNOTATION	RHYTHM
CONSONANCE	RHYME
COUPLET	SATIRE
ENJAMBMENT	SCANSION
EPIC	SIMILE
EPITAPH	SONNET
FIGURATIVE LANGUAGE	STANZAS
FOOT	SYLLABLE
HAIKU	SYMBOL
HYPERBOLE	SYNECHDOCHE
IMAGERY	TANKA
IRONY	TERCET
LIMERICK	THEME
LINE	UNDERSTATEMENT
LYRIC	VERSE
METAPHOR	VILLANELLE

Additional Terms

Choose as many additional terms as you would like and write them in the squares. Repeat each as desired.
Cut out the squares and randomly distribute them to the class.
Instruct the students to place their square on the center space of their card.

© Barbara M Peller

Clues for Additional Terms

Write three clues for each of your additional terms.

_____ 1. 2. 3.	_____ 1. 2. 3.
_____ 1. 2. 3.	_____ 1. 2. 3.
_____ 1. 2. 3.	_____ 1. 2. 3.

Roses are red, Violets are blue, Sugar is sweet. And so are you.	Roses are red, Violets are blue, Sugar is sweet. And so are you.	Roses are red, Violets are blue, Sugar is sweet. And so are you.	Roses are red, Violets are blue, Sugar is sweet. And so are you.	Roses are red, Violets are blue, Sugar is sweet. And so are you.
Roses are red, Violets are blue, Sugar is sweet. And so are you.	Roses are red, Violets are blue, Sugar is sweet. And so are you.	Roses are red, Violets are blue, Sugar is sweet. And so are you.	Roses are red, Violets are blue, Sugar is sweet. And so are you.	Roses are red, Violets are blue, Sugar is sweet. And so are you.
Roses are red, Violets are blue, Sugar is sweet. And so are you.	Roses are red, Violets are blue, Sugar is sweet. And so are you.	Roses are red, Violets are blue, Sugar is sweet. And so are you.	Roses are red, Violets are blue, Sugar is sweet. And so are you.	Roses are red, Violets are blue, Sugar is sweet. And so are you.
Roses are red, Violets are blue, Sugar is sweet. And so are you.	Roses are red, Violets are blue, Sugar is sweet. And so are you.	Roses are red, Violets are blue, Sugar is sweet. And so are you.	Roses are red, Violets are blue, Sugar is sweet. And so are you.	Roses are red, Violets are blue, Sugar is sweet. And so are you.
Roses are red, Violets are blue, Sugar is sweet. And so are you.	Roses are red, Violets are blue, Sugar is sweet. And so are you.	Roses are red, Violets are blue, Sugar is sweet. And so are you.	Roses are red, Violets are blue, Sugar is sweet. And so are you.	Roses are red, Violets are blue, Sugar is sweet. And so are you.
Roses are red, Violets are blue, Sugar is sweet. And so are you.	Roses are red, Violets are blue, Sugar is sweet. And so are you.	Roses are red, Violets are blue, Sugar is sweet. And so are you.	Roses are red, Violets are blue, Sugar is sweet. And so are you.	Roses are red, Violets are blue, Sugar is sweet. And so are you.
Roses are red, Violets are blue, Sugar is sweet. And so are you.	Roses are red, Violets are blue, Sugar is sweet. And so are you.	Roses are red, Violets are blue, Sugar is sweet. And so are you.	Roses are red, Violets are blue, Sugar is sweet. And so are you.	Roses are red, Violets are blue, Sugar is sweet. And so are you.

Acrostic
1. In this type of poem the first letters of each line usually spell a word or name.
2. In this type of poem the first letters of each line may list spell out a message.
3. "A Boat, Beneath A Sunny Sky" is one. Found in Lewis Carrol's *Through the Looking Glass*, the first letters of each of its lines spell out Alice in Wonderland's real name.

Allegory
1. It is a story with two meanings, a literal meaning and a symbolic meaning.
2. Like a symbol, it conveys abstract ideas to get a point across; however, it differs from a symbol in that it is a complete narrative.
3. Dante's *Inferno* is an example of this extended metaphor.

Alliteration
1. It is the repetition of consonant sounds.
2. The repeated consonant in this sound pattern usually comes at the beginning of words.
3. "While I **n**odded, **n**early **n**apping" from Poe's "The Raven" is an example of this.

Allusion
1. This is a reference in a literary work to something outside of the work.
2. If you referred to someone as a Scrooge, you would be using this literary device.
3. John Milton's epic poem *Paradise Lost* has many; most refer to th Bible.

Assonance
1.It is the repetition of vowel sounds within non-rhyming words.
2. An example of this poetic device can be found in Poe's "The Bells.*"* An example is the phrase "Fr**o**m the m**o**lten-g**o**lden n**o**tes."
3. Another example of this device from "The Bells,*"* by Edgar Allan Poe, is this line: "Hear the m**e**llow w**e**dding-b**e**lls."

Ballad
1. It is a type of narrative poetry. In other words, it tells a story.
2. The Scottish poem "Barbara Allen" is a famous example of a folk ____.
3. This type of poem is often set to music. Before the time of books, musicians went from town to town and sang them.

Caesura
1. It is a brief pause that breaks up a line of verse.
2. In scansion it is shown by the use of a double virgule (//).
3. The following line from a poem by Emily Dickinson has an example of this type of break in a line of poetry: "I'm nobody! Who are you?"

Cinquain
1. It is a five-line poem.
2. The lines have the following number of words: one word, two words, three words, four words, and one word.
3. Often the word in the fifth and final line of this poem is a synonym for the word in the first line.

Clerihew
1. It is a short, humorous, biographical poem.
2. These humorous poems have an *aabb* rhyme scheme.
3. The first line names a person, and the second line ends with something that rhymes with the name of the person.

Connotation
1. It is the associated meaning of a word or a phrase.
2. An antonym is *denotation,* or the clearly expressed meaning of a word or phrase.
3. The word *slender* has a positive one for most people; the word *skinny* has a negative one for most.

Consonance 1. It is the repetition of consonant sounds within words. 2. It differs from alliteration because of the position of the repeated consonant sounds. 3. Although the repeated sounds can come in the middle of words, it often refers to the ending sounds, such as *note, bat,* and *set.*	**Couplet** 1. It is made up of two lines that rhyme and have the same meter. 2. Two lines of verse that act as a unit. 3. Chaucer's *Canterbury Tales* is written in rhyming ones. An example follows: "The tender shoots and buds, and the young sun Into the Ram one half his course has run…"

Enjambment
1. It is the continuation of a sentence from one line or couplet into the next.
2. The term derives from the French word *enjamber,* meaning "to straddle."
3. Joyce Kilmer uses this technique in his poem "Trees." Note the continuation.
    ""I think that I shall never see
    A poem lovely as a tree."
	Epic
	1. It is a long narrative poem.
	2. *The Iliad* and *The Odyssey,* by Homer, are examples.
	3. Virgil's *The Aeneid* is one; so is John Milton's *Paradise Lost.*

Epitaph 1. It is a short text inscribed on a tombstone. 2. This one is on the Tomb of the Unknown Soldier: "To save your world you asked this man to die: Would this man, could he see you now, ask why?" 3. Winston Churchill's says, "I am ready to meet my Maker. Whether my Maker is prepared for the great ordeal of meeting me is another matter."	**Figurative Language** 1. In this type of language the words and phrases go beyond their literal meanings. 2. Simile, metaphor and personification are three common types of this kind of language. 3. Idioms are a form of this type of language.
Foot 1. It is the unit used in poetry. Examples are iambic, trochaic, anapestic, dactylic and spondaic. 2. An iambic one consists of two syllables; the accent is on the second. 3. A trochaic one consists of two syllables; the accent is on the first.	**Haiku** 1. ___ and tanka both originated in Japan, but the tanka is longer. 2. This Japanese poem has three unrhymed lines of five, seven, and five syllables. 3. This 3-line Japanese poem form is often used to reflect on an aspect of nature. Its name means "play verse."
Hyperbole 1. This figure of speech is an exaggeration. 2. If your friend says to you, "I tried to call you a million times," it is an example of this. 3. Referring to a tornado as "a little wind" is ___. Elements of Poetry Bingo	**Imagery** 1. This refers to the use of descriptive language that appeal to the readers' senses. 2. It is language that stimulates one or more of the senses: hearing, taste, touch, smell, or sight. 3. These phrases in "Preludes," by T.S. Eliot, are examples: *stale smells of beer, sawdust-trampled street, muddy feet,* and *raising dingy shades."* Note how they appeal to the senses. © **Barbara M Peller**

Irony
1. It refers to how something is not as it seems. There are several types, including verbal, dramatic and situational.
2. Verbal ___ is the use of words to express something other than and usually the opposite of the literal meaning. Sarcasm is an example.
3. Situational ___ is an outcome contrary to what was or might have been expected.

Limerick
1. This type of five-line, humorous poem was popularized in English by Edward Lear in his *Book of Nonsense,* written in 1845.
2. This humorous five-line poem has one couplet and one triplet. It has an *aabba* rhyme scheme.
3. Edward Lear wrote 212 of these humorous poems. Each was accompanied by a humorous illustration.

Line
1. Also called a verse, it is measured by the number of feet.
2. Pentameter is the name given to one with 5 feet. Hexameter is the name given to one with 6 feet. It is also known as a verse.
3. Hexameter is the name given to one with 6 feet. It is also known as a verse.

Lyric
1. This poetry has the musical quality of a song.
2. This song-like poem is written to express emotions or thought. It is relatively short.
3. The sonnet is a type of ___ poem. An elegy is a mournful one written in memory of someone who has died.

Metaphor
1. This is a comparison between two unlike things without the use of *like* or *as.*
2. This figure of speech says something *is* something else when in reality it is not.
3. An example of this figure of speech is in this line of poetry by Emily Dickinson: "My Life had stood—a Loaded Gun." She compared her life to an unused loaded gun.

Meter
1. It is the basic rhythmic structure of a verse and is defined by the number of feet and the accent pattern.
2. Dactylic hexameter was the ___ used by Homer and Virgil.
3. The most common ___ in English verse is iambic pentameter.

Metonymy
1. This refers to the substitution of one term with another loosely associated with that term.
2. "The pen is mightier than the sword" is one. The word *pen* has been substituted for "written words that express thoughts" and the word *sword* has been substituted for "military action."
3. The use of the term "the Crown" to represent a king or queen is an example of this.

Ode
1. These long, serious poems originated with the ancient Greeks. Those that model Pindar are structured. The English form is more irregular.
2. The Greek poet Pindar (c. 522 BCE to 443 CE), wrote many in honor of excellent athletes.
3. Keats, Byron and Shelley perfected the form of English ones. "___ on a Grecian Urn, written by Keats" in 1819, is a well-known one.

Onomatopoeia
1. This refers to the use of words that sound like the sounds they describe.
2. Use of words such as *buzz* and *hiss* are examples of this.
3. In "The Bells" Poe uses this device to let us hear the different kinds of bells: *tinkling* sleigh bells, *clanging* fire bells, *chiming* wedding bells and so on.

Parody
1. This is a work that imitates another work for a humorous or satirical effect.
2. It is sometimes colloquially referred to as a "spoof."
3. It imitates an existing work, usually by exaggerating its characteristics, to make fun of it. It is related to satire.

Elements of Poetry Bingo

© Barbara M Peller

Personification
1. It is the bestowing of human qualities on inanimate objects, ideas and animals.
2. "The sun peeped into the window" is an example of ___.
3. This excerpt from *Oliver Twist,* by Dickens, is an example of ___: "There are smiling fields and waving trees."

Poet
1. It is a person who writes poetry.
2. Keats, Byron and Shelley were famous English ones.
3. Carl Sandburg and Robet Frost were famous American ones.

Poetry
1. Along with prose, it is a major division of literature. It has more structure than prose.
2. A novel is a form of prose, but an epic is a form of this.
3. This broad type of literature uses sound and rhythmic language to evoke an emotion.

Quatrain
1. It is any four-lined poem or stanza of a poem.
2. It is the most common stanzaic form in the English language.
3. Four possible rhyme schemes for this type of poem are *aabb, abab, abba,* and *abcb.*

Rhythm
1. It is the pattern of strong and weak sounds.
2. We say it is falling ___ if stress occurs regularly on the first syllable of each foot.
3. We say it is rising ___ if stress occurs regularly on the last syllable of each foot.

Rhyme
1. It is the correspondence of terminal sounds of words or of lines of verse.
2. The words *book* and *look* ___.
3. Two possible ___ schemes for quatrains are *aabb* and *abab.*

Satire
1. It is a literary work that pokes fun at individual or societal weaknesses.
2. Although this literary genre is usually meant to be funny, its main purpose is to attack something of which the author disapproves.
3. In this genre the author uses wit and humor to poke fun at something and show disapproval.

Scansion
1. It is the system of marking metrical patterns of a line of poetry.
2. This process of dividing a verse into its metrical components is sometimes called scanning.
3. In ___ a caesura is indicated by a double virgule (//).

Simile
1. It compares unlike things using *like* or *as.*
2. This figure of speech says something is like something else though the two are quite different.
3. Examples are in this stanza by Robert Burns:
*"O My Luve's **like a red, red rose,***
That's newly sprung in June;
*O My Luve's **like the melodie***
That's sweetly played in tune."

Elements of Poetry Bingo

Sonnet
1. It is a 14-line poem written in iambic pentameter.
2. Two main kinds are the Petrarchan, or Italian, and the Shakespearean, or English.
3. "How do I love thee? Let me count the ways..." is a famous one by Elizabeth Barrett Browning.

Stanzas	**Syllable**
1. It is a fixed number of lines of verse that form a unit of a poem; they are named according to the number of lines they contain. 2. Prose is divided into paragraphs; poetry is divided into ___. 3. A couplet is a 2-line one; a tercet is a 3-line one; a quatrain is a 4-line one; and so on.	1. It is a unit of spoken language. 2. A haiku has 17. 3. A tanka has 31.
Symbol	**Synechdoche**
1. It is an object, character or idea that is used to represent something else. 2. It associates two things, but unlike a metaphor, its meaning is both literal and figurative. 3. Robert Frost used this in "The Road Not Taken." The forked road represents the choices we have in life.	1. It is a figure of speech in which a part stands for a whole or vice versa. 2. Using the USA to stand for the athletes who actually won in "The USA won ten gold medals in today's events" is an example. 3. Saying "All hands on deck" to tell all sailors to report to duty is an example.
Tanka	**Tercet**
1. It is a poem with 31 syllables arranged in groups of 5, 7, 5, 7 and 7. 2. This form of poetry and haiku both originated in Japan, but the haiku is shorter. 3. It is similar to haiku but has more syllables and uses simile, metaphor and personification.	1. It is a three-line poem. 2. It has one more line than a couplet. 3. A haiku is an unrhymed one.
Theme	**Understatement**
1. It is the main idea of a literary work—the idea the author wants to convey. 2. The importance of family is a common one. 3. Good versus evil is a common one.	1. This is the stating of something less strongly than the facts seem to warrant. 2. To say "it's rather breezy" during a hurricane would be an example. 3. A litote is a form of this.
Verse	**Villanelle**
1. A single metrical line of poetry is called this. 2. Sometimes this word is used as a synonym for the word *stanza*. 3. Free ___ does not follow any metrical pattern. Blank ___ has a metrical pattern but is unrhymed.	1. It is a nineteen-line poem with two repeating rhymes and two refrains. 2. It comprises five tercets and a quatrain. 3. A well-known example of this nineteen-line poem is "Do Not Go Gentle into That Good Night," by Welsh poet Dylan Thomas (1914–1953).

Elements of Poetry Bingo

Elements of Poetry Bingo

Scansion	Acrostic	Alliteration	Hyperbole	Assonance
Foot	Allegory	Understatement	Parody	Stanzas
Theme	Onomatopoeia		Rhythm	Verse
Tercet	Sonnet	Tanka	Ode	Poet
Quatrain	Limerick	Epic	Symbol	Metaphor

Elements of Poetry Bingo: Card No. 1

Elements of Poetry Bingo

Tercet	Theme	Lyric	Simile	Metonymy
Poet	Epitaph	Cinquain	Sonnet	Poetry
Connotation	Limerick		Line	Tanka
Rhyme	Satire	Onomatopoeia	Villanelle	Assonance
Stanzas	Understatement	Epic	Foot	Symbol

Elements of Poetry Bingo

Limerick	Tanka	Epitaph	Ode	Theme
Poet	Allegory	Clerihew	Acrostic	Irony
Sonnet	Understatement		Poetry	Allusion
Onomatopoeia	Connotation	Quatrain	Rhyme	Lyric
Symbol	Consonance	Epic	Villanelle	Metonymy

Elements of Poetry Bingo: Card No. 3

Elements of Poetry Bingo

Onomatopoeia	Poetry	Alliteration	Consonance	Metonymy
Personification	Caesura	Acrostic	Simile	Theme
Rhythm	Rhyme		Metaphor	Hyperbole
Tanka	Onomatopoeia	Understatement	Epic	Cinquain
Couplet	Stanzas	Ballad	Symbol	Verse

Elements of Poetry Bingo

Stanzas	Assonance	Sonnet	Cinquain	Consonance
Personification	Tanka	Clerihew	Line	Allegory
Alliteration	Verse		Parody	Imagery
Metaphor	Metonymy	Scansion	Villanelle	Enjambment
Epitaph	Epic	Theme	Onomatopoeia	Rhythm

Elements of Poetry Bingo

Allusion	Poetry	Lyric	Metonymy	Verse
Ode	Sonnet	Enjambment	Acrostic	Theme
Simile	Couplet		Caesura	Line
Epic	Quatrain	Villanelle	Ballad	Alliteration
Poet	Cinquain	Scansion	Rhythm	Figurative Language

Elements of Poetry Bingo

Scansion	Poetry	Imagery	Tanka	Epitaph
Poet	Metonymy	Limerick	Allegory	Personification
Lyric	Hyperbole		Line	Caesura
Onomatopoeia	Rhyme	Clerihew	Tercet	Connotation
Epic	Consonance	Villanelle	Ballad	Allusion

Elements of Poetry Bingo

Rhythm	Poetry	Haiku	Ode	Caesura
Personification	Alliteration	Simile	Verse	Cinquain
Figurative Language	Consonance		Metonymy	Assonance
Symbol	Onomatopoeia	Tercet	Couplet	Rhyme
Understatement	Epic	Ballad	Sonnet	Poet

Elements of Poetry Bingo

Line	Epitaph	Limerick	Figurative Language	Consonance
Couplet	Metonymy	Rhythm	Sonnet	Poetry
Irony	Scansion		Allegory	Haiku
Enjambment	Assonance	Quatrain	Parody	Imagery
Rhyme	Villanelle	Clerihew	Tercet	Metaphor

Elements of Poetry Bingo

Tercet	Ode	Caesura	Simile	Figurative Language
Verse	Cinquain	Acrostic	Allegory	Metonymy
Consonance	Poetry		Hyperbole	Connotation
Quatrain	Metaphor	Enjambment	Villanelle	Irony
Clerihew	Poet	Lyric	Stanzas	Rhythm

Elements of Poetry Bingo

Allusion	Poetry	Sonnet	Enjambment	Poet
Haiku	Irony	Parody	Line	Acrostic
Personification	Metonymy		Lyric	Limerick
Clerihew	Theme	Villanelle	Consonance	Tercet
Couplet	Epic	Scansion	Ballad	Epitaph

Elements of Poetry Bingo

Epitaph	Assonance	Irony	Ode	Line
Limerick	Poet	Alliteration	Ballad	Allegory
Scansion	Imagery		Verse	Simile
Epic	Rhyme	Metonymy	Tercet	Personification
Poetry	Haiku	Consonance	Couplet	Cinquain

Elements of Poetry Bingo

Enjambment	Assonance	Allusion	Irony	Verse
Alliteration	Haiku	Metonymy	Line	Connotation
Ode	Cinquain		Limerick	Imagery
Rhythm	Villanelle	Caesura	Consonance	Tercet
Epic	Metaphor	Ballad	Scansion	Parody

Elements of Poetry Bingo: Card No. 13

© Barbara M Peller

Elements of Poetry Bingo

Foot	Metonymy	Sonnet	Line	Couplet
Cinquain	Scansion	Irony	Allegory	Poetry
Enjambment	Hyperbole		Lyric	Clerihew
Metaphor	Villanelle	Consonance	Caesura	Allusion
Epic	Simile	Connotation	Poet	Rhythm

Elements of Poetry Bingo

Parody	Line	Sonnet	Epitaph	Ode
Allusion	Lyric	Acrostic	Alliteration	Couplet
Verse	Scansion		Theme	Poetry
Epic	Irony	Haiku	Villanelle	Enjambment
Poet	Rhyme	Ballad	Figurative Language	Limerick

Elements of Poetry Bingo

Caesura	Irony	Haiku	Figurative Language	Satire
Simile	Connotation	Imagery	Personification	Hyperbole
Enjambment	Assonance		Verse	Limerick
Onomatopoeia	Cinquain	Epic	Parody	Tercet
Couplet	Synechdoche	Ballad	Rhyme	Poetry

Elements of Poetry Bingo

Clerihew	Syllable	Meter	Irony	Foot
Parody	Couplet	Villanelle	Hyperbole	Imagery
Line	Rhythm		Synechdoche	Haiku
Metaphor	Poet	Tercet	Sonnet	Connotation
Quatrain	Enjambment	Epitaph	Ode	Assonance

Elements of Poetry Bingo

Figurative Language	Consonance	Cinquain	Enjambment	Simile
Poetry	Clerihew	Quatrain	Verse	Couplet
Line	Connotation		Meter	Alliteration
Assonance	Acrostic	Villanelle	Tercet	Lyric
Synechdoche	Irony	Sonnet	Syllable	Allusion

Elements of Poetry Bingo

Verse	Allusion	Irony	Haiku	Tercet
Parody	Ode	Poetry	Epitaph	Hyperbole
Syllable	Consonance		Allegory	Theme
Lyric	Synechdoche	Quatrain	Rhyme	Meter
Alliteration	Satire	Poet	Rhythm	Ballad

Elements of Poetry Bingo: Card No. 19

Elements of Poetry Bingo

Foot	Syllable	Ode	Irony	Ballad
Cinquain	Limerick	Personification	Quatrain	Simile
Assonance	Imagery		Onomatopoeia	Acrostic
Stanzas	Understatement	Symbol	Rhyme	Synechdoche
Tanka	Rhythm	Satire	Tercet	Meter

Elements of Poetry Bingo

Parody	Allusion	Personification	Irony	Stanzas
Assonance	Meter	Caesura	Haiku	Scansion
Connotation	Poet		Syllable	Sonnet
Quatrain	Epitaph	Synechdoche	Metaphor	Rhythm
Onomatopoeia	Satire	Ballad	Clerihew	Rhyme

Elements of Poetry Bingo

Figurative Language	Lyric	Meter	Alliteration	Enjambment
Simile	Ode	Theme	Haiku	Allegory
Cinquain	Hyperbole		Scansion	Imagery
Synechdoche	Metaphor	Rhyme	Acrostic	Personification
Satire	Clerihew	Syllable	Connotation	Lyric

Elements of Poetry Bingo: Card No. 22

Elements of Poetry Bingo

Caesura	Syllable	Epitaph	Alliteration	Ballad
Allusion	Foot	Poet	Parody	Acrostic
Lyric	Enjambment		Symbol	Scansion
Connotation	Satire	Synechdoche	Clerihew	Rhyme
Stanzas	Understatement	Rhythm	Quatrain	Meter

Elements of Poetry Bingo

Caesura	Rhythm	Foot	Syllable	Haiku
Meter	Ballad	Personification	Simile	Scansion
Imagery	Figurative Language		Enjambment	Connotation
Stanzas	Symbol	Synechdoche	Clerihew	Assonance
Tanka	Onomatopoeia	Satire	Ode	Understatement

Elements of Poetry Bingo

Onomatopoeia	Personification	Syllable	Sonnet	Meter
Acrostic	Assonance	Parody	Caesura	Allegory
Metaphor	Haiku		Symbol	Synechdoche
Theme	Stanzas	Understatement	Satire	Hyperbole
Ballad	Foot	Cinquain	Couplet	Tanka

Elements of Poetry Bingo

Meter	Syllable	Lyric	Simile	Figurative Language
Quatrain	Ode	Haiku	Foot	Caesura
Metaphor	Symbol		Hyperbole	Onomatopoeia
Clerihew	Alliteration	Stanzas	Satire	Synechdoche
Imagery	Couplet	Sonnet	Understatement	Tanka

Elements of Poetry Bingo

Lyric	Cinquain	Syllable	Foot	Limerick
Stanzas	Symbol	Parody	Synechdoche	Allegory
Villanelle	Understatement		Satire	Onomatopoeia
Figurative Language	Allusion	Personification	Tanka	Acrostic
Couplet	Hyperbole	Meter	Theme	Imagery

Elements of Poetry Bingo

Lyric	Foot	Theme	Syllable	Caesura
Limerick	Meter	Symbol	Simile	Hyperbole
Understatement	Connotation		Imagery	Quatrain
Tercet	Figurative Language	Poet	Satire	Synechdoche
Alliteration	Line	Couplet	Tanka	Stanzas

Elements of Poetry Bingo

Meter	Foot	Figurative Language	Parody	Line
Rhyme	Quatrain	Personification	Imagery	Theme
Metaphor	Symbol		Allegory	Syllable
Limerick	Stanzas	Metonymy	Satire	Synechdoche
Caesura	Haiku	Tanka	Allusion	Understatement

Elements of Poetry Bingo: Card No. 29

© Barbara M Peller

Elements of Poetry Bingo

Consonance	Syllable	Simile	Line	Synechdoche
Acrostic	Foot	Lyric	Hyperbole	Allegory
Metaphor	Enjambment		Imagery	Personification
Tanka	Allusion	Alliteration	Satire	Symbol
Stanzas	Verse	Understatement	Meter	Theme

© **Barbara M Peller**

www.ingramcontent.com/pod-product-compliance
Lightning Source LLC
LaVergne TN
LVHW061337060426
835511LV00014B/1971